The Sestina Playbook

by
Jules Nyquist

Poetry Playhouse Publications
Placitas, NM

The Sestina Playbook
Copyright 2020 by Poetry Playhouse Publications,
Placitas, NM
ISBN: 9798621632588

Font: Century Gothic and Calibri

Cover & inside photos by Jules Nyquist
Cover Design Denise Weaver Ross

All rights reserved. This book, or sections of this book, may not be reproduced or transmitted in any form whatsoever without written permission from the publisher. jules@poetryplayhouse.com
www.poetryplayhouse.com

dedicated to:
the master troubadours

The Sestina Pattern

STANZA I		...new order...	STANZA II III IV V VI
end-word	1	2nd	6 3 5 4 2
	2	4th	1 6 3 5 4
	3	6th	5 4 2 1 6
	4	5th	2 1 6 3 5
	5	3rd	4 2 1 6 3
	6	1st	3 5 4 2 1

1 2 3 4 5 6 – Stanza A
6 1 5 2 4 3 – Stanza B
3 6 4 1 2 5 – Stanza C
5 3 2 6 1 4 – Stanza D
4 5 1 3 6 2 – Stanza E
2 4 6 5 3 1 – Stanza F
(6 2) (1 4) (5 3) – Envoi,
or the "grand finale"

Copy this page and paste it somewhere where you can reference it when you have the urge to write a sestina! Put it on your phone notes, take a photo of the form, carry this book around with you. You never know when you will need to reference the sestina form in your writing.

The Sestina Pattern as Labyrinth

I like this form so much I'm making a labyrinth out of the sestina pattern in the Jules' Poetry Playhouse backyard.

TABLE OF CONTENTS

Why form? Why six?	1
Dear Sestina (letters)	3
The Troubadours	5
Write Your First Stanza	7
School	8
Exercise 1A	10
Exercise 1B	11
Choosing your Teleutons	14
Exercise 2	16
What do the Teleutons say?	18
Veronica	19
Exercise 3	22
Obsessive Content	23
Roses	24
Exercise 4	27
The Meditative State	28
A Kind of Courage	29
What is It?	31
Exercise 5	33

Mirroring	34
Somewhere	35
Intrepid	38
Exercise 6	40
A Long Attention Span	41
Radium Girls	42
Day One	44
Exercise 7	46
Humor & Politics	
A Sestina for the Way Social Conservatives Want Americans to Have Sex	47
American Blackout	51
Teleutons Chosen by Others	53
Punk Band Tours the Galaxy	54
Exercise 8	57
Line Length	58
Brewery	59
Malan	61
Exercise 9	63
Odes & Letters	
Ode to Erica Jong	64
North Korea Hwasong-15 Shrine	67
Dear Dirty Dublin	69
Exercise 10	71
Collaboration and Character	72
A Sestina for Susan	74
Exercise 11	77

The Envoi	78
Exercise 12	79
Sestina Variations: Tritina	80
Featheridge	81
Mating Rituals	82
Half Sestina, Double Sestina	83
Double Sestina in Fiction	84
Exercise 13	85
Dear Sestina revisited	86
Exercise 14	87
Sestina References by the Author	90
For Further Reading	92

Why form? Why six?

Sestina – Italian sesta (sixth)

Sestina is Italian for *sesto,* which means sixth. The sestina is a long, usually narrative poem that provides structure for obsessions or emotional complexities. It is six stanzas of six lines, plus an envoi (last stanza) of three lines, with a total length of 39 lines. The end words repeat in a set pattern and are called teleutons. The length of the lines can be short or long, but usually follow an iambic pentameter pattern. Length is usually consistent in a single poem, but not always.

The sestina can be a lonely form, as not all poets want to attempt them. Having support of other poets helps to generate new poems. Share this book with friends to start your own sestina group, or sign up for a Jules' Poetry Playhouse class on sestinas at www.poetryplayhouse.com. If your poet friends scoff at attempting a sestina, don't be discouraged. You have this playbook to help you construct your own sestinas. There seems to be a tight clique of poets that like to write in form.

"A sestina can be an embarrassment to formalists," says James Cummins.
          Do you ever consider yourself a formalist? asks Jules.

> "That is a fraught question! I struggle with that all the time...you try to do the thing that's true to you and your way of saying things...the discipline. I think of it as wrestling, the kind of competition with form. That form makes you better."
>
> *Jules Nyquist interview excerpt with sestina poet James Cummins*

One book that changed my life on sestina writing, and why I am obsessive about it, is *Jim and Dave Defeat the Masked Man* by James Cummins and David Lehman. It is a comic-style book with illustrations for each sestina. Teleutons have variations with names of poets as end words, or dialogue variations, breaking rules and having a lot of fun. Cummins and Lehman wrote the poems but did not disclose who the author was for each poem except at the end of the book, where the contents section is really an envoi.

I had the pleasure of interviewing James Cummins by phone for my lecture research during grad school at Bennington College and am indebted to him for sharing his thoughts with me. James wrote another amazing book, *The Whole Truth* which is one long epic poem, composed of 24 sestinas in sequence with a plot line like a mystery novel. This was Cummins' first book of published poetry!

What are my students saying about the sestina form? At the end of the six-week sestina class that I teach, I had my students write the sestina a letter. Here is a sampling:

Dear Sestina:

I love that your formal name is like the name of a female friend or relative (I cannot imagine writing to anyone named Ode, Sonnet, or even Villanelle). You have been with me these six weeks, and allowed me to spend time with you, bringing a new energy to my writing. I cannot say it will create a lasting change--that remains to be seen--but I have a new appreciation for your form. I like the look of you, the math of you, the length, width, depth, and the path of you. Silliness aside, you have taught me that my rants can be honed into poetry, and that an idea worth having also bears repeating.

Your sister in poetry,

    Andi Penner, Albuquerque

P.S. I love knowing that you'll always be 39!

Dear Sestina,

Your ancient form, your quirky structure and your playfulness, have taught me not to take myself so seriously. You have shown me that words in and of themselves, can lead to words outside of themselves, to ideas that would not have blossomed had your six-stanza form, your teleutons and your eclectic jovial challenges, not forced me to banter words around until they exploded into concepts that were sparked deep in the recesses of my mind.

Thank you for surviving the ages,

*   Joanne Bodin, Albuquerque*

Sestina, you six-headed monster,

No sooner do I cut off one head, then you grow six more, forcing me to play your game until I come close enough to cleave you in half.

*   Denise Weaver Ross, Albuquerque*

The Troubadours

Arnaut Daniel, 12th Century poet and mathematician

The invention of the sestina is usually attributed to Twelfth Century Italian poet Arnaut Daniel, a Twelfth-Century poet and mathematician. Daniel referred to what we call a sestina as "cledisat", meaning, more or less, "interlock." (1)

Arnaut Daniel was one of the first troubadours, which is based on the French verb, *trobor,* which means "to invent or compose verse." The first sestinas were written in Italian, Portuguese and French. The first English sestina showed up in 1579. I encourage you to research more history on your own, as there are many sources to consider.

The Troubadours were performing poets traveling for their fame and fortune to shock, delight and entertain their audiences. Troubadours also sang: their poems were usually accompanied by music, and they were known for performing in the courts of royalty. They competed with one another to produce the wittiest, most elaborate, most difficult styles of poetry. The sestina was the form for a master troubadour. I hope I have done it justice; I am just beginning to discover its many pleasures of obsessive repetition.

I like to think of the original sestina troubadours, including Daniel, as the original "slam" poets. They challenged themselves to invent more complex forms of poetry, as well as to entertain.

Of course, once you know the rules of the sestina, you can very them, and break them. The possibilities are as endless as the sestina itself, folding and weaving its fascinating form into endless variations.

(1)- https://en.wikipedia.org/wiki/Sestina

*The sestina is a form
like a thin sheet of flame,
folding and infolding
upon itself.....*

Ezra Pound

Write your first stanza

backwards and forwards triads

6 1 5 2 4 3

pairs adding to 7

Six words are chosen and occur as end words in each line, and repeat themselves in a set order in each stanza. The last word of the end line of the one stanza is repeated as the last word of the first line of the next stanza, technically rhyming with themselves.

There are a couple of different ways to start a sestina. Some poets like to choose their six words in advance and write the first stanza using those words. Others may want to write a stanza with six lines and then see what those end words turn out to be, and use those end words as the teleutons for the sestina. Whatever way you choose, experiment! You'll have many exercises to practice your sestina writing. The first recorded sestina words are said to be: *soul, chamber, nail, uncle, rod, enter,* recorded by our first sestina troubadour, Arnaut Daniel, written around 1200 AD.

Let's start with my sestina *School:*

School

or will clouds
cluster
to cover
her &
the blue wind
gather at her

shoulders she
reads Erica Jong under cloudy
skies, wind
popping clusters
of couples together &
under cover

of trees over
muted her
professors lecture &
she'll never get clouds
of science bluster
to unwind

her windy
classmates, undercover
crushes fish cluster
in schools girls unlike her

all clouded
with mascara &
faces to the winding
long road of Beatles cloud
bearing songs to cover
scratched heart, she
clusters

by herself, clustering
couples under &
below trees under her
favorite branches water wind
around her cover
homeroom clouds

endless cluster of names her
body cloudy &
small covering wild wind

What are the six end words?
What are the teleuton variations?

Teleutons: clouds/cloudy/clouded, cluster/clusters/clustering, cover/over/bluster, &, wind/windy/unwind/winding, her/she

**Exercise #1A
Write your first stanza**

1. Think of six words you'd like to use as teleutons. Use them to write a first stanza.

2. Now, write another stanza on the same subject, not paying attention to the end words. Where would you put the line breaks? What words would you use as teleutons?

Compare your two versions. What do you like best? You are free to choose your teleutons from here. Be sure these are the ones you want, as your form will progress in the sestina pattern from this point forward.

Exercise #1B
Write your sestina

　　　　　1 2 3 4 5 6 – Stanza A
　　　　　6 1 5 2 4 3 – Stanza B
　　　　　3 6 4 1 2 5 – Stanza C
　　　　　5 3 2 6 1 4 – Stanza D
　　　　　4 5 1 3 6 2 – Stanza E
　　　　　2 4 6 5 3 1 – Stanza F
(6 2) (1 4) (5 3) – Envoi, or the "grand finale"

Using your first stanza, from the first part of this exercise, write it out labeling each line with the end words assigned a number. I have used my poem *School* as an example. Use YOUR first stanza when you fill in the blanks.

　　　　　clouds　　　1
　　　　　cluster　　　2
　　　　　cover　　　3
　　　　　&　　　　　4
　　　　　wind　　　　5
　　　　　her　　　　6

Now you have numbered your teleutons (end words). Repeat the end words for the remaining five stanzas. I like to take a blank sheet of paper and write ONLY the end words out, repeating the pattern. This is my framework for the rest of the poem.

6 1 5 2 4 3 – Stanza B

    she   6
    cloudy   1
    wind   5
    clusters 2
    &   4
    cover   3

3 6 4 1 2 5 – Stanza C

    over   3
    her   6
    &   4
    clouds   1
    bluster   2
    unwind`   5

5 3 2 6 1 4 – Stanza D

    windy   5
    undercover 3
    cluster   2
    her   6
    clouded 1
    &   4

4 5 1 3 6 2 – Stanza E

&	4
winding	5
cloud	1
cover	3
she	6
clusters	2

2 4 6 5 3 1 – Stanza F

clustering	2
&	4
her	6
wind	5
cover	3
clouds	1

(6 2) (1 4) (5 3) – Envoi (any order)
in this poem I used cluster 2, her 6
cloudy, 1 &, 4
covering, 3 wind, 5

If things don't work out as planned, that's okay. Sometimes a poem isn't meant to be a sestina. Even if it isn't finished, you'll have some word combinations that you may not have come up with, which may work for the poem in another form.

Choosing your teleutons

There can be a trick to choosing words that have potential for variations. What words make the best teleutons? If a word can be spelled or used in more than one way, it can be easier to work with. Common words such as their/there/they're or two/too/to have a lot of possibilities. Don't overlook common words such as "the" or "and." Variations such as fast/breakfast add dimension. Another language can be used for the same word, such as dog/perro.

Some of my favorites used in my poems in this playbook include:

zip/zipless/zipper
feather/plume/quill
writers/writes/writing
love/amour
dog/perro
tooth/toothbrush
thankful/full/fully
BASIC/basic
poison/poised
because/pause
construction/construct/reconstruction
tea/coffee
heat/humidity
fish/salmon

We will explore more teleuton variations in a later chapter, but for now, pay attention to what words work for you. You may want to challenge yourself with the longer word combinations (such as construction/construct/reconstruction) listed above. I've also tried more uncommon words such as American, abortion, responsible, Pogue! (using an exclamation mark for punctuation).

**Exercise #2
Collect teleutons**

I've started collecting words that may be future teleutons. This way, I have a sample to choose from if I'm not yet ready to write a poem. A fun way to do this is to use index cards. These can be used as playdecks, or pocket inspirations. I credit this idea from writer Miriam Sagan, mentioned in her book: *Unbroken Line: Writing in the Lineage of Poetry*(Sherman Asher, 1999).

I also personally "collect" words from various sources, including magazines (cut out the word and past on an index card), (I'm a big fan of collage), or in my on-line subscriptions to "word of the day" types, I'll jot down intriguing words that may have more than one meaning or variation. You can even browse the dictionary.

Write down several words you may want to use as future telutons. You may want to use index cards, or list them on paper, allowing space between each word. Then explore the variations on the words you choose.

Examples:

    zip/zipless/zipper

    feather/plume/quill

What do the Teleutons say?

When the end words say something (a secret code) they are part of the poem but also have a meaning all their own, separate from the poem. There are a few examples of this, my favorite being Miller William's "The Shrinking Lonesome Sestina" which says in its teleutons, "time goes too fast, come home." William's line lengths go from long to progressively short, which also shows us the shortening of his memories, which adds to the impact of the poem.

In my sestina, *Veronica,* you can find the message: love is a dog from hell (in tribute to Charles Bukowski's collection).

Veronica

On a Mexican Faster Sunday, love
will only torture Veronica. She is
chained to the bed like a dog,
silver dish tipped over, perro,
running from
that future hell.

Why does a stranger run through hell
to save a half-faced baby dog
born on the beach in low tide? Is
it a piece of broken pottery, loved
only by its mother, running from
the children? Run, perro

run. Run across history. Run, perro
run. Veronica hides her love

in seawater, believes it is
safe to swallow salt. Hell
is losing herself to the wild dog-
faced priest who enters her from

his own lost place, from
the way he tries to take her with him. Isolation is
a mannequin with a doll's face. One blind dog
leads her, but beware the perro
that will nip at her heels and bite her neck. Hell
is remembering fragments of love,

and why he once loved
her, before the unborn baby became an inferno
between them. When it is midnight, flying perro
bats circle around her and the priest in bed. Veronica is
not afraid, she is calm from
their silent wings, their gray dogged

dives. Her priest is full of his own dogma
as he climbs out of bed and cannot love
her anymore. The Pacific pulls her under. She is
swimming with her clothes on. Half a doll's head
appears from
under a wave and she sees her own face. An inferno
of laughing children swim beside her. Wild perro

dogs release her from his illicit love. The priest is in his
own hell.

Tomorrow his face will plaster the Mexican papers
and her body will be found, cut into pieces. Run, perro
run!

Sestina for Veronica Andrade Salinas, the victim of the Easter killing in Toluca, Mexico by Cesar Torres, a Catholic priest. She died April 16, 2006.

Note: the second stanza is 6,3,2,1,5,4 instead of 6,1,5,2,4,3. My variation.

**Exercise #3
Teleutons that say
something**

Write a sestina with teleutons that say something. For example, in "Veronica", the six words are: *love, is, dog, perro, from, hell*. (Love is a dog from hell was inspired by the title of the book by Charles Bukowski). *Hell* and *inferno* are also used interchangeably, and words may include variations *(dog, dogma, dogged)*.

Obsessive Content

> *A closed form for a powerful voice –*
> *the incantatory dramatics of the recurring end-*
> *words haunted and challenged me.*
> Honor Moore

My poem *Veronica* from the previous chapter is also an example of obsessive content that can be carried using the sestina form as a type of scaffolding. This scaffolding is where you, as a poet, can hang emotions, language and desires. The sestina challenges the poet to meet its subject in an obsessive, repetitive form.

One example I use in my classes is Honor Moore's "First Time, 1950." How would a topic like domestic abuse and violence be different if the form was not a sestina?

Another topic that lends itself to obsession and repetition, which can be difficult to write about, is death. I wrote this sestina, *Roses*, about my Mom's unexpected death. I worked in elements such as roses (which my mother loved, and my Dad loved to grow in his garden), a vegetable (corn, one of my Dad's favorites) and the kitchen table, which triggered a lot of family memories.

Roses

Dad picks roses
for Mom from
the garden to put
in a vase on her table
but by end of April the snow
swept up the cornstalks

the latest anyone with corn
had seen snow, the roses
covered the doorstep the snow
didn't get to and from
Dad's parent's kitchen table
he looked out at his dad putting

the stalks upright, he put
the yellowed leaves of stalks

that would come back, tabled
around after the sun rose
again blooming, going from
spring and planting to snow

within a week of snow
it melted and the corn was off, put
back on track from
seasons into growing corn
knee-high by July 4th, rising
up for glory, tables

of produce, sweet corn tabled
under melting snow
but we can't eat roses
we can only put
them out as a memorial to lost corn,
lost names, lost graves from

one city to the next, from
moving the family farmhouse table
moving the whole house surrounded by corn-
fields where little boys grow up to shovel snow
and fix semi-trucks, work construction, put
food on the table with a vase of roses

in the middle for Mom, covered from snow
her table set for guests that never came, put
out the corn, the butter, the salt, the roses.

**Exercise 4
Obsessive content**

Think of a topic that you've been wanting to write a poem about that is difficult for you to talk about or approach. Maybe you've tried to write about it before, but the poem isn't going anywhere. See if the sestina form can help you. Start with your first stanza and see where the teleutons take you. You may be surprised by where they lead you.

You may also want to include concrete descriptions in your sestina, such as a flower, a vegetable, and what happens around a table.

The Meditative State

The poet and photographer Star Black has some wonderful interpretations on the magic of the sestina. I interviewed her in grad school and she told me about how she writes double sestinas (which use 12 teleutons, 12 stanzas and a 6 line envoi!) and she remarks it was a bit like weaving a blanket. You know how you're going to end with the form, but you do not always know what you are going to say.

For me, the sestina form is almost like a meditative state, where it pulls me off base, asks me to write the first stanza without restraint and then write into the form. The meditation of the form releases the poem that is waiting to be written.

I like to start with a question. I wrote on the question: *"What kind of _____ is it?"* I then added an object (pottery) and a color (blue). I wove these items into the theme of the poem in my sestina, *A Kind of Courage*.

A Kind of Courage

What kind of courage is it?
The anxious, scary kind,
the pottery on her aunt's shelf in turquoise blue
chipped on the rim, well-worn and loved
through three generations and now you are responsible
for keeping it safe, handling it to save your life.

What kind of fool takes their life
and leaps into their unfamiliar? It's
a congested kind of dust responsible
for new allergies, a woman who never knew the kinds
of desert plants that would settle into her love
of chamisa, blooming yucca, juniper and incredible blue

sky, blue hovering sadness, blue
disappearing into the Great Lakes. Her life
out of the fog of waiting. How she loved
seeing Dad at the kitchen table, six am, it
was him alone, eating breakfast cereal, kindness
in his hands as she joined him, responsible

for getting up for school, responsible
with Mom and brother still in bed, her blue
eyes join his dream world of working trucks, kinds
of home calling her away even then. Life
someday giving her offices, cubicles, typewriters, it

never stopped with just carbon paper and blue stencils
loved

by her Mom's church secretary upper office, love
of the smell of mimeographed bulletins responsible
for news and prayer chains and the next holy season, it
churns them out around the wheel of yellow, blue,
purple, pink and red. She waits for her life
to arrive at the front steps, waits for the boy on the
motorcycle, kind

of coming to pick her up, where they kind
of talk and lay down in the green park grass where love
eludes her young body this time. Life
will grow on in years, waiting to be responsible
for her own wedding crystal, her own blue
sky over her grandmother's lost grave in Iowa, it

takes her prairie life and leads her. A kind
of courage, it gives her love of the wind,
her response to chipped blue pottery.

I used this same question on another poem of mine,
What Is It? asking "What kind of balance is it?" using
the object shattered glass and the color red.

What is it?

What kind of balance is it
that shatters like glass
flows like a river of red
bloody or joyful?
Her mood of the day
(daring or shy) depends

on nothing. A hawk depends
on wind to glide it
doesn't worry day to day
about what is broken glass
anxious about a full
cup or a half, red

or blue. She mostly feels red
disappears into edges that depend
on others not seeing her full
of flowers in a blue vase. It
helps to wear dark glasses
when outside during the day.

What kind of day
is it when she sees in red

and breaks her glasses
blurry vision, it all depends
on devices to aid her, help it
all along as she ages. Thankful

for friends, living parents, a full
heart of a man loving her day
by day the balance swings, it
turns solid, then liquid, then red
gas, blood, flowing or not, depends
if she's in menopause or not, glass

ceiling in career, breaking glass
gives her strength, she can joyfully
do whatever she wants. Deepens
with every year. The days
have no names, no numbers, they only redden
as a rash overtakes her. It's

time to depend on a smooth glass table
cover it with fabric, full of
dishes by day, read books at night.

**Exercise 5
Meditative state with a question**

Write a sestina asking the question: "What kind of ____ is it?" where the blank is something that you want to discover in your poem. (balance, courage?) It can be abstract or more concrete, and hopefully something that you want to dive into. Once you have that question as the first line of your poem, add in an object, and a color and see where the sestina takes you.

Mirroring

> *The teleutons of the fifth stanza are not the teleutons of the first, though they hang the same way over the bridge-rail.*
>
> Ezra Pound

A master troubadour will make a sestina look easy. It will build upon itself. One way to think about this is "not stepping into the same stanza twice." (James Cummins). The poet James Cummins, who was one of my mentors in researching sestinas, remarks in his essay "Calliope Music: Notes on the Sestina" (Antioch Review Vol. 55 #2, Spring 1997), that "basic to the sestina form are issues of time, the voyage out, the return, change, repetition-as-development, self-reference, self-consciousness. Evidently, these early poems were accompanied by a dance." Cummins also mentions, "..the sestina is not a lyric form, though it has lyric aspects. It is a meditative, narrative, dramatic form, and we need to adjust our ears to hear it today."

I had the pleasure of interviewing Jim Cummins by phone for my lecture research and I am indebted to him for sharing his thoughts with me. Cummins' says that you can go over all the rules you like, to try to master the sestina form. Mastering, however, is not how one goes about writing a sestina. It can master you. What poets think of the sestina is almost as obsessive as the form itself.

In the following sestina of mine, *Somewhere,* I used the first stanza of Margaret Atwood's poem *Daybooks 1,* as the first stanza and let the teleutons take me where they needed to go.

Somewhere

This is the somewhere
We were always trying to get:
Landscape
Reduced to the basics:
Rolling mills, rocks, running
Water, burdocks, trees living and dead. (1)

Somewhere the dead
are buried under humps of dirt, somewhere
a white cross perches with faded plastic flowers run
over on the highway by drivers who will rush to get
somewhere unimportant. A basic
necessity of burial: warm landscape

soft enough to dig. We walk the land, scope
out our future with planted trees, no dead
ancestors among us. Basic
survival skills are burdock roots, some

flower stalks harvested before they get
to bloom. Tree bark stripped off as runners

to make canoes, stone faces stare at us from the bank.
We run
into landscape.
Some day we will elope to a new place, get
dressed in red and tie ourselves to trees. The dead
and living surround us. Somewhere
in our pockets lie changes. BASIC

programs run on a green screen. Basic
codes run all life forms. Somewhere someone runs
deep into the forest. Ferns unfold. Some ask where
they are but we see another landscape
appear on the screen. Death
sleeps under down covers. No graveyards to get

creepy with. Graves are fine and private, we get
consolation in the land of Elysian, a basic
right of passage with manicured lawns, the dead
no longer gone but sweetly singing under running
water, weeping willows, the statuary landscape
attracting tourists with guidebooks, draped urns,
winged cherubs, somewhere

over the rainbow death got lost.
This is the somewhere we exit, back to basics.
Run to the stonecutter, chisel our own mortality.

> (1) Opening stanza quote is verbatim from "Daybooks 1,"
> Two Headed Poems, Margaret Atwood 1978.

"The mirror image 'rhymes' with itself but is not 'itself.' The telutons are signposts – each time you come around them you are made aware…of the passage of time….Each teleuton must change, grow, contain more or other than its previous incarnation, whit it contains its own echo, another fascinating aspect of rhyming itself." (Cummins, Calliope).

As the words went around the labyrinth of the six stanzas, they evolved into a reminiscing of mixed memories into one large image. Each time a word comes around on the sestina pattern, it is the same, yet new. Our walk through the labyrinth is a bit like the sestina pattern. The same path comes around again, but we are changed, we've progressed into something different even as we see the same rocks, the same dirt. Yet it is not perfect, it is more like conversation, offering new insights each time. Sometimes it works beautifully, sometimes it doesn't. After a third or fourth stanza with the teleutoms coming around, if we don't have that sense of growth or moving on, the sestina can flop. Obsession has to drive the form and the subject, and also a bit of playfulness.

This sestina mulls over the end words: intrepid, that, tourist, solo, naked, stars and their variations. It is far from perfect, but I share it here as an example of the sestina form taking me on another one of it's journeys around the labyrinth. The first stanza of my poem *Intrepid* uses the title as the first line.

Intrepid

was it that
blind touristy
feeling? I slept over solo
in Taos in a tent on a cot naked
under night stars

I'm the star
of my own life, intrepid
walk to the outhouse naked
feel the vastness that
really is, a solo
truth, no more tourist

skimming sights, touristy
fearless stupidity under stars
hiking arroyos solo
or driving a Mustang intrepidly
to the man-cave that
got a guy stuck, naked

tires in the deep snow, nude
horizons where a tourist
is saved by a Zia Pueblo native that
used chains to get him to star
back for his own intrepid
poetry reading, a solo

performance, like wild horses, solo
words of truth, spun naked
into tales of unrequited intrepid
hauntings, a tourist
gone mad under the stars
sets a glass on the family piano, that

party where she is told that
we are all here solo
to make what we see in a star,
every night, bears and bobcats hunt naked
in the mountains; coyotes stalk a tourist's
dog downtown, an intrepid

poet orders a scotch straight up, a waitress that
gets it wrong, adds ice, she asked for no ice, solo
a naked tourist caught up in the wildness.

**Exercise 6
Mirroring**

Select a favorite poem that represents obsession. Use the first stanza, or first line to start our sestina. What appeals to you about the poem you selected? How will you break the lines and choose your teleutons? Be sure to give credit to the author.

How is mirroring reflected in your sestina? See how your teleutons progress through the sestina pattern and come out changed. Did the poem go where you wanted it to? How have you changed along with the sestina on its journey?

A Long Attention Span

The sestina's long form of 39 lines may not be used to what we hear in today's texted, shortened, short attention-span world. But when we let the sestina take us obsessively and repetitively to deeply explore those emotions and observations, we are along for the ride. The teleutons mirror and reflect various meanings and we can have fun with the form, even if we are writing about difficult subject matter.

The sestina's long form gives us a chance to explore a subject in depth in a way we may not in a shorter form. The form can hold us accountable to asking the hard questions and expand that meditative space, especially if it is a subject that the poet feels needs more attention and space, such as *Radium Girls.*

Radium Girls

They promised you the glamour kiss
and more money than you'd ever know
a chance to be an "artist"
with a watch on everyone's wrist, a cause
to be proud of, the glow
of radium dials, a poison

of occupational radiance, poised
to point your paint brushes for a kiss
on your lips, that finer point, a better glow
on your face, you painted unknowingly
your fingernails, your toes, a manicure that causes
you heartache, for the love of the art.

You were mistaken, self-luminous art
disintegrates your marrow, hollow poisons
cake your eyelids, yet you see fireworks, cause
cataract meteors to burst, flash and kiss
your retinas, radiant light emitting knowledge
like a forbidden apple, a glow-

worm-like heat, ionic energy glows
with phenomenal brilliance and ecstasy, art
in its deadly, fullest knowledge
reveals the secrets of Marie Curie -- not poison,
but a miracle cure for everything, a radiant kiss

of luck for bath salts, chocolate, *Radithor* bottled water
        -- because

water is better than Radium beer; pause
with your man at the Radium Palace Hotel, it attracts
        the glow
of 2500 customers a year, the price kissed
up to 3000 times the worth of gold, an artist
could splurge while working in radium, its delicate
        poison
like a lover that seduces without protection, you know

you shouldn't but you do, what do you know
that could possibly go wrong? You didn't sue because
only later you found out it was poison
to ingest like a bitter apple, that warm glow
on your face, your teeth falling out, your art
becoming a frail, old woman after being kissed

too many times by her lover, you knew all along the
        glow
was temporary, caused by cruel greed, cheap women
        artists like you
used up and only the men got autopsies, you kissed
        away your future.

The long attention span can also be used to tell a story, as the sestina uses a narrative form. Political issues asking tough questions are a topic that can be handled with a sestina, since the end words repeat the obsessive issue that the poem explores. My poem *Day One* addresses Dr. Robert Oppenheimer, father of the atomic bomb.

Day One

Day one
the big bomb to win
the war of wars, the big
one, how many times
do you think, Doctor?
The Army wants to know!

Dr. Oppenheimer says he knows
the gadget will work and be one
big blast (in his doctoral
opinion), a dud would not win
us anything, we need more time
to develop a device that's big

enough to blast a whole city, the biggest
bomb yet. No one says no.
The lure of the times
of mastering physics, one
more secret revealed to stroke and win

our American egos, scientists being doctors

of chemistry, mathematics and physics, doctors
of humanity, push forward to big
revelations, patriotic to win
against Nazi Germany, to know
they are helping the war effort, one
time for them to go down in history, time

to do something at Los Alamos. Timeless
beauty surrounds the doctors
in sky and pines, the mountains the one
source of exclusive secrecy, so big
no outsider knows what's on the Hill, no
leaks on the big day when the test wins,

blasts out at Trinity. The crew cheers, we win
our intellectual battle of energy and time.
Now the Army takes ownership, knows
we have leverage to bomb the Japs, Dr.
Oppenheimer has done his job, big
plans to drop the device within one

week to win the war. The newspapers now know
America counts one sole time victory.
No more big secrets, Doctor, how do you feel?

**Exercise 7
Long Attention Span**

Use your 39 lines to deeply explore a topic. What will the teleutons mirror and reflect as you explore your observations and emotions? Don't be afraid to dive into a political or personal topic that you feel passionate about.

Humor

When writing about heavy topics, such as politics, sometimes it's best to lighten up. Choose some challenging teleutons that have many syllables and go together with the sounds in your mouth that you like to say. You'll be repeating them a lot. I had some fun with the next poem, using teleutons: abortion, contraception, bedroom, sex, Christian and virgins.

Sestina for the Way Social Conservatives Want Americans to Have Sex

Eventually, all roads
lead to abortion.
The war on
contraception
starts in your own
bedroom.
What goes on between
American husbands and wives having sex
is now monitored by self-appointed Christian
morality police. They roam the land, preying on
      unsuspecting virgins

who pledge a vow of abstinence before marriage. Do
      the virgins
reveal that they're still virgins to their future husbands?
      Is contraception

allowed in the bed? No! shout the Catholics, it's a form
    of abortion,
it prevents a future life, which starts at implantation,
    not birth. The bedroom
is no place for fun, no place to be physical! Hell no, the
    fetus is part of your sex
life! The fetus will have full legal status, including the
    right to choose, say Christian

social conservatives. South Dakota has confirmed that a
    Christian
fetus just made a decision to kill its mother. It will be
    born in her bedroom
while she goes into a coma and dies shortly after the
    birth. Virgins
will help deliver the baby, which will grow up to be a
    terrorist with an anti-abortion
agenda. Fathers everywhere say this is a step forward to
    equality in contraception.
The women have held the advantage for too long. Soon
    fathers will also have sex

for the sole purpose of getting pregnant. New drugs are
    on the way to adapt the male sex
drive away from having sex without the intent to
    procreate. The bedroom
used for enjoyment is a very bad thing. It should be
    turned into a nursery with proper Christian

heroes decorating the walls. Adam, Noah and Abraham
    are a good start. They lusted after virgins,
tried to kill their first born sons and would have never
    subjected their sixty-year old wives to
    contraception.
But then, they didn't have to worry about HIV, STD's
    and the FDA. Abortion

wasn't legal then, and the social conservatives want to
    make sure it never will be again. Abortion
can only hurt the rise of the male phallus. Women have
    too much say already. Sex
for enjoyment is for sinners. Sex with the same sex, sex
    with condoms, sex with virgins,
sex with other races, sex with no insurance, sex outside
    of marriage, sex toys and sex with non-
    Christians
is all forbidden. Women will have no money, no jobs,
    no freedom and if they cannot have children
    born in their bedrooms,
they will die. A Protestant American couple avoided
    contraception

and used in-vitro fertilization. They were showing off
    their twins on CNN. No contraception
is good, said the Catholic priest, but an un-natural birth
    is bad, so they were fired from their jobs,
    aborted

just like that. The priest went on to say that good
          Christian
mothers don't breast feed their babies either. There is
          evidence that virgin
milk from a breast feeding mother has a contraceptive
          effect so a woman can have sex
and not get pregnant. That's just as effective as the pill,
          the IUD or Plan B. A special press conference
          was held in the White House bedroom

to address the topic once and for all. Mr. President, do
          you support the right to use contraception? He
          was asleep in the bed.
The First Lady replied instead: "I haven't had
          sex with him for years, so there can be no
          chance of any abortions.
I was a virgin when we met. We are good Christians."

                              photo credit, Jules Nyquist,
                              Acapulco, Mexico mannequins

In this next poem I draw from personal experience using unique teleutons to channel range into form.

American Blackout

Teeth and claws
are necessary in society. That's the American
way. Tina and Clay sit on the fire escape by a heap
of ashes. The blackout
made them reinvent
their evening. BBQ grill yes. Electric tooth-

brush, no. Tina's dentist raves about the sonic tooth
brush. What is society coming to? American
health insurance with no dental coverage. Clawing
in a cubicle for eight hours a day. Heaped
on the couch, blacked out,
exhausted. There has to be a way to reinvent

a life. Fuck the Americans. Clay reinvents
himself every winter in Mexico. No Americans.
No electricity. Manual tooth
brush. If there was a blackout,
no one would notice. They'd claw
around for the next Pepsi, heap

themselves on sand by the beach. Heaping
steaming piles of raw meat. Teeth
full of fire. Reinvented

stories passed down by black birds, claws
clenched to carry away the gringos, Americans.
America needs another blackout,

Tina remarks. Blackout
the damn TV's for 24 hours. See if Americans
fall apart. Reinvent
themselves on boredom with teeth-
grinding anxiety; they'll have to heap
themselves with entertainment, claw

out of the black hole they've clawed
themselves into, grind their teeth
as they all drive out of town for gas, heap
on the anti-depressants, reinvent
their CD collection for cash, pray the blackout
doesn't last another minute. Americans

will die in the desert. Tooth, claw
and reinvented wheel. Tina and Clay heap
on another beer, toast to an American blackout, soon.

Teleutons Chosen by Others

I was feeling a bit lonely in my grad school residency and had friends send me their favorite groups of six words. Some came by email, and some by postal letter. It was fun to see what words were chosen, handwritten on an index card or typed electronically. I tried to use these words to inspire me. If you want to get to know your friends, neighbors, or strangers; ask them to write down six random words. Whatever words you choose, choose carefully as you will be using variations on these words for six stanzas, plus the envoi, or last stanza of three lines, gathering all six words together.

On the same theme, I also tried using words that were unusual, in my poem *Punk Band Tours the Galaxy*, such as Pogue! and included the exclamation point. See how many unique words you can use. This poem includes: scrim, double, punk, galaxy, gas, pogue!

Punk Band Tours the Galaxy

In a room with no words, scrim
divides the love seat from the double
purpose stage. The musicians filter in. Punk
rock, gypsy punk, they play a galaxy
of hot tunes, cut the fool, gas
up desire on the front line. Pogue!

They play Bjork, Gogol Bordello, fuck, even Madonna -
    pogue!
Outside, angry, bored workers and doubly
bored teachers escape to Lunds. They gas
up the Saab, play the band's latest gypsy punk
on the iPod and puree a fruit smoothie in the Galaxie
blender. Sushi to go. Scrim

won't keep the lovers apart. Scrim
clothing makes a statement on the drummer as he
    doubles
on another beat. The toy accordion diva finds another
    galaxy

of tunes with no words between her and her fans.
   Pogue!
Nothing sex has turned to chaos, punk
love and sushi.com. Gas

is four dollars a gallon. Wars for gas
still clutter the galaxy.
Sex is illegal. The doubles
partners hide under their hats of chaos, Pogue!
Even kissing can be useful for faking marriage between
   scrim
halls. To avoid the cameras, get punk,

play it out with a pun.
Music hides a double
knowledge of language. The band will gas
up with latex gloves and plastic scrim
hides them from their fans. Pogue!
The lead guitar player rules the galaxy,

shouts sounds and wordless strings to vibrate galactic
gigantic raps! He jumps, punked
and galiant! He is an Alcatraz flowering. Pogue!
Later, when he is arrested for truth, he is not afraid of
   scrim
veils on a president's face, but gas
will kill three women in a car, a double

collision. Pogue! Terrorists rush the scrim, try to save the women, duel with no words. They fire gas bullets to ban the music. The world is punked. Hurry, save the galaxy!

**Exercise 8
Humor & Teleutons
Chosen by Others**

Experiment with your teiutons! Have a friend write six words for you and see what you an come up with for a new sestina. Or, if you are looking to have something in the mail or on line, suggest friends send or post six words and you may have an unending source of material for teleutons and sestinas!

Write a sestina with a sense of humor.

Line-length

Length is usually consistent in a single poem, but not always. One example I use a lot is Miller William's "The Shrinking Lonesome Sestina" where the line lengths start out long and then get shorter with each stanza, with the last stanza just one word for each stanza. An extra layer of dimension is that the telutons spell a phrase.

In my *Brewery* sestina, I started writing this at a Brewery in Albuquerque, on bar coasters and napkins, noting observations, drinking root beer. Of course, the six telutons here are: soul, out/out-(cast), meet, beer/beers, band/band-(width), sound/sounds. Note how you can hyphenate words like out-cast and band-width to divide themselves on different lines. I also eliminated the stanza breaks, which helps the flowing effect.

Brewery

one soul
ventures out
to meet
for a beer
and a band
Jesse the sound
man makes sounds
groove to soul
music, the Broken Rule band
plays too loud; out-
casts, we are. no beer
for her, she meets
him by the bar, meets
to get away from sounds.
orders 2 root beers
texts another soul
to embark out-
side to see this band,
it's worth at least a band-
width, a molecule meets
another homonuclear couple, out
where the sounds
are gathering oxygen, souls
talking, ordering beers,
but it's not about the beer
or the background band
it's about the souls

gliding in to meet
a perfect rhythm of sound
bytes, coming out
on the dance floor out
with strangers, a beer
cannot be sent through sound
waves into a band
on his finger to meet
his other half, a soul
mate, out with the band
where a beer meets a nucleus
soundlessly in the palm of a soul.

A sestina can also start out with one word for each line, and then gradually grow longer stanzas, like a flower unfolding. In *Malan,* the city name is the name of a flower, and the metaphor plays well to the growing nuclear test base.

Malan

Chinese
desert
flower
unfolds
to blossom
Mao's A-bomb

His wish for a bomb,
a nuclear weapons test base, China's
is seven times bigger, blossoms
over the U.S. test base in the Nevada desert.
The Great Leap Forward unfolds
starving workers eat the wild flowers

Malan is named for a desert flower
rising from the ashes of a future bomb
a new town of ten thousand people unfolds.
With help from the Soviets, China
rises her pioneer ashes out of her desert,
to assemble thousands of workers, blossoms

to resurrect Cheng Ho's Fifteenth Century, blooms
fleets of sailing treasure ships, flowers
spreading inventions of Second Century paper desert
origami birds, gunpowder bombs
once the largest navy in the world, China
rises again, magnetic stones, compass-like, unfold

to tell her future. Mao's wish unfolds,
an A-bomb test within ten years to blossom
(with three months to spare) the People's Republic of
          China
joins the nuclear club on October 16, 1964. A white
          rose flowers
in history, the giant physics experiment blows
up, forced to bloom from the Lop Nor desert.

Testing blossoms for 32 years with desert
detonations, the first one code named "596" unfolds,
is named after June 1959, the time when the bomb
given to China from the Russians and blossomed
in trade for Tibetan uranium, turned into a wilting
          flower
suddenly cut off by Khruschev. So China
builds her own bomb, lighter and better than the U.S.
          Desert
winds and Chinese fortunes willed to unfold.
At what price blooms Malan in the parched desert?

**Exercise 9
Line Length**

Write a sestina with no more than four or five words for each line, paying attention to how the words look on the page. If appropriate, you can also eliminate the line breaks between stanzas to further "hide" the sestina form.

A second exercise would be to play with the line lengths, starting out short and growing long, or the opposite, like a flower folding in or opening up. What can the lines represent as it fits into your subject?

Odes

An obsessive form, the sestina can be a great form for your ode. One of my favorite authors is Erica Jong and this sestina makes a political statement with some humor.

Ode to Erica Jong

> *"It was not the sex the puritans*
> *hated and feared. It was the abundance.*
> *It was not the four-letter words;*
> *it was the five-star soul."*
> *--Erica Jong on Henry Miller*
> *(from "The Devil at Large")*

Solitude is un-American.
How can a single
girl compare her sex
life with a man's, when he zips
out his desire and writes
about it for the next best-seller? Fall

down on your knees, girl. Zippers fall
away like rose petals, single
women everywhere unzip
their men to reveal American
underwear blown off in a breath. Sex
like dandelion fluff. You write

"Fear of Flying" in 1973, writing
to break women free, not some sexy
chick lit. This is the zip-
less fuck. Faceless, ordinary accidents. Americans
pretend not to notice dark falls
into tunnels with strangers. Single

or married, man or woman, does a single
gender matter? Does love even have a sex?
If one is lucky enough to fall
in love, who cares what sex the zip-
per unzips? As writers,
we are paid for our pain and our un-American

nightmares. Heresy in America
is choosing to be single,
to *not* be part of a couple. We hunger to fall
in love. We drift foggily from writing
at the desk to aching for sex
and yet, when we get it, unzip

it all and throw it out, another zip-
less fuck. Isadora wonders: why do Americans
say they hate pleasure? Why do they fall
down to work endlessly, to barely write
a word and single
out those who will not be slaves? To talk about sex

zips their mouths closed. Sex in a dark age turns
		Americans bitter.
Presidents go blind and empires fall. His wife, a former
		librarian,
gives up the classics and can't recall a single word.

A more contemporary political poem follows in this reflection on what one country uses for a shrine. The varying line lengths give it texture.

North Korea Hwasong-15 Shrine

> *North Korea was so proud of missile,*
> *it got its own shrine.*
> *New York Times Headline, March 18, 2018*

missile
park
construction
is huge
North Korea is proud!
What is going on?

Swarms of tiny U.S. satellites suspected something
going on
a throne to the Hwasong-15 missile
snapshots show a shrine proud
with propaganda, a memorial park
carved out of farm fields, huge
trucks crawling with construction

digging gear, crews and reconstruction
to honor a missile? What is going on?
Our spies are baffled by a huge
parking lot. Is it meant for a missile

museum? A memorial park?
An astonishing achievement, shroud
in secrecy, unveiled to a crowd,
spy satellite snapshots show construction
of a shrine, a massive missile park.
What is going on?
First one built to be able to hit the U.S., a missile
memorial to the phallus, a huge

stadium being built, another huge
area for fireworks, loud
sirens announcing the missile
liftoff, on display to construct
the mirage going on
a light show in the dark

crowds gather in the park
for Kim Jong-un, not a stooge
to them, or to admit what is really going on
North Koreans must act proud!
This site is pretty, with landscaped construction,
even a commemorative postage stamp for the missile

to send censored mail, those in the park are proud
of huge, hand-constructed masturbation manipulation
What the hell is going on with their missiles?

An ode can also be in the form of a letter. I wrote this letter to the city of Dublin, and included some of the favorite food items I thought represented my visit to the city.

Dear Dirty Dublin:

Your emerald sparkle is lost in humidity
as we are welcomed with scrambled eggs, coffee,
scones and an assortment of jams from a dispenser;
        tea,
of course, everywhere to my delight, salmon
and fruits, a buffet of desires, pubs

around the corner, too early for the pub
Guinness on tap, but everyone here smokes and Dublin
is heavy on the meat. Cows in the fields see the fish
in our eyes and no more sleeping in a tent for you! The
        heat
is unusual for July, but at *Books Upstairs*, tea
is still properly served upstairs. I like my coffee
black; you have your rich cream, a cappucino

or latte, or a flat white. The gray men already in pubs
with warm beer, brown grass, dark tea
and gray sky; homeless in the streets. Dublin's
many bridges over the River Liffy soar over my hot
flashes that follow me as we search for the best fish

and chips. You like peas on the side, I prefer fish
only and just the chips please, no more espresso,
too hot, no air conditioning; sweat it out in humidity
to meet your friend at that famous Mulligan's pub
and that time both soccer teams partied, not knowing
who won in Galway (not Dublin),
jammed in at the bar. *Sláinte!* I escaped to my tea-kettle

in the hotel room, no fragile teacups,
only the glass of the grandmothers, who prepare broiled fish
with yolks of eggs, or make sweet smelling scones; a rainy Dublin
day over Mrs. Mooney's butcher shop, reading books and drinking coffee
in her kitchen with scandalous Bob who came in from the pub
to propose to her daughter Polly, who is upset with his hot, sweaty

hands. It is you, dear dirty Dublin, you are adored through the choking humidity,
coffee nightmares and overbearing tea, the endless pubs to crawl, steamy fish tales and right now we need a good gelato!

Yours truly

**Exercise 10
Odes & Letters**

Write a sestina in the form of an ode, or a letter, sense of humor, or not. Use the examples from this chapter as ideas. Is there a person or object that is worthy of an ode?

Is there a place or a person that you can write a letter?

Collaboration and Character

As I mentioned in the first chapter, James Cummins wrote a book "The Whole Truth" which is one long epic poem. My dear friend Susan Paquet wrote her own six-act sestina murder mystery, "Barrio Streets," a chapbook starring Gloria, Dolores, Celestina, Rita, Marisela and Agraciana as the main characters, each with their own sestina adventure.

Susan Paquet was a master sestina writer and to honor her, our writing group (of which she was a part) wrote a collaborative group sestina. Susan was dying of ovarian cancer. She courageously planned a farewell party on her birthday in July because she wanted to remember her friends and life with the joy that she gave so many of us. So the three of us in our group, Andi, Joanne, and I, sat down at the classroom of Jules' Poetry Playhouse in the summer of 2018 and wrote "A Sestina for Susan" in about an hour or so. This was when Jules' Poetry Playhouse was located on Granite, between 5th & 6th streets on the edge of downtown Albuquerque.

The three of us worked on the first stanza together. We each wrote a line, or collaborated, and agreed on the telutons, which wound up being "love, home, mystery, recipes, barrio and goat." They were reflective of our thoughts about Susan, and were fairly common words we thought we could use in writing our own stanzas, with a sense of humor. It would be challenging to use "goat" six times, but that was part of the fun, and we knew Susan would enjoy reading whatever we came up with.

Susan owned three goats: Hyacinth, Daisy and Rose and a large poodle named Asta, which are referenced. She previously owned dog, cats and a donkey. Susan was an attorney specializing in adoption and her husband Andy was retired and baked delicious apricot empanadas. Her murder mystery sestina was set in the barrio, and Mrs. Basetti was a character in her novel of stories *Rocky Mountain Recipes for Murder: Historical and Personal Tales from Pueblo, Colorado* (Mercury Heartlink) that she had published, but unfortunately, had to cancel the book launch planned at Jules' Poetry Playhouse because she was too sick. This sestina honors Susan and was healing for the three of us dealing with our grief.

After the first stanza, we each wrote two stanzas (2nd and 3rd, 4th & 5th, 6th and envoi). We spent about a half hour silently writing our stanzas and then came together to see what we wrote and agreed that this is what worked, with some minor edits. We read the sestina as a group to Susan at her party that July.

A Sestina for Susan
by The Crosstown Poets (Jules Nyquist, Andi Penner & Joanne Bodin)

Knowing Susan has been a festival of love,
a cross-town bus toward home
and a humorous, gracious, bell-bottomed mystery.
We gathered around poetry and shared recipes
for life – to persevere, be happy and never forget the
        barrio
where Celestina walks the street while Daisy (the goat)

looks at her through the fence, wondering what kind of
        goat
she is. Susan writes through eyes of love –
portraits of friends, family, pets and barrio
neighbors, wherever she calls home;
whether Pueblo, El Paso, or Albuquerque. Her recipe
for happiness is the same: family, laughter and mystery.

Her life is a sensory experience, a world filled with
        mystery.
Tie-dyed colors, writing paper for poets and goats.
Susan writes about her husband's mother's recipe
for apricot empanadas. Andy bakes them with love
for his wife, his sweetheart, the light of his home
where we meet from across the barrio.

We burn our own Zozobra in the barrio
He fizzles and smokes, we feed him our mysteries,
hopes and fears. Andy and Susan travel to their El Paso
    home
where the windows to Susan's imagination opens. The
    goats
are not there but she loves them as family, her true
    amour
around the kitchen table with music and good recipes.

Mrs. Basetti's potato sandwich recipe
was shared by lawyers in el Barrio.
Susan writers murder mysteries with love,
delicious Sicilian spaghetti tales of mystery,
apricots and tortillas eaten by the goats
Hyacinth, Daisy and Rose and poodle Asta at home.

Born in July with fireworks and apple pie, Susan came
    home
into the arms of her parents, her grandmother's recipe
box of treasures and family photos – always the goats,

dogs and cats and even a donkey living in the barrio.
Susan seeks diversity in speaking Spanish and sharing
tie-dyed dime story mysteries,
always tempered with her inimitable sense of humor
    and love.

People in the barrio love a good mystery.
How simple life can be at home with a book
filled with good recipes and paper for the goats to eat!

**Exercise 11
Collaboration**

Think of someone who you could honor, remember or get to know better with a sestina. How can you include details of their life in your stanzas? What telutons can you use that describe this person? You can collaborate with others in the actual writing of the sestina by sharing stanzas, or you could interview others about the person and bring in different viewpoints.

The Envoi

We now come to the last stanza, which is called the envoi. We have worked our way around the labyrinth…..and if we had a seventh stanza it would take us around to our original teleutons pattern (ABCDEF or 123456). Again, the sestina surprises us. It does not have a full seventh stanza, it has a truncated final stanza using all six words in three lines, wrapping up in an envoi. the sestina is full of surprises, defeating our expectations as we jump off the end of the poem making a bit of a statement as we finish into a "grand finale" that can be subtle, or not.

The sestina is how we wrap up to take the weaving off the loom, the yarn off the needles, how we jump off the bridge into what is next. We step out of the labyrinth in a graceful, or surprising way as we wrap up the poem. The poem that has us wrapped up in itself.

(6 2) (1 4) (5 3) – Envoi

**Exercise 12
The Envoi**

Experiment with some envoi variations in your sestina.

You do not have to use this exact order! As long as you have all six teleutons preferably spaced out in three lines for your last stanza, you've got a wrap.

Sestina Variations

There are, of course, many variations of the sestina pattern. Once you master one, you can create another. To know the rules and then break them, you can create new forms of your own.   Here are a few variations.

Tritina

The Trintina is attributed to poet Marie Ponsot (20th Century) which is a contraction of the sestina form using three line stanzas and one concluding envoi.

First stanza: ABC teleutons
Second stanza: CAB
Third stanza: BCA
Envoi: ABC repeated words in the final line can be in any order.
(ABC and 123 are interchangeable)

I came across the tritina much later than my discovery of the sestina, and it's a perfect form for beginners, or for when you want a shorter jump into the water. Kind of like the kiddie pool, or staying on the shallow end. Yet, it is still a very powerful form. I've included it at the end of this book since it is a variation of the sestina. Here are two that I've attempted.

Featheredge
> *in memory of poet Stewart Warren*

You seem more comfortable with stars
my first glance of you at Aceqiua Books, your feathered
hair hangs over eclipsed eyes

and you were just down from El Rito, or maybe seen
in Carbondale. Both of us new to 'Burque, you suggest
        Flying Star*
insist on hearing my journey, but a feather

in your cap I'm not. I invite your plumed
wings to rise early with ballooning, grey eyes
rising, closer to a shattered moving sun

You gather entourages, make keen-eyed introductions
wrap me up with a nova man and a wedding blanket
exploding poems in your quill

*Flying Star is the name of an Albuquerque restaurant chain

In *Featheredge,* I broke the tritina envoi rule and used three lines as an envoi. In *Mating Rituals,* I've followed the one line envoi including the three teleutons.

Mating Rituals

The antics of our neighbor's male roadrunner
has him rejected; he has no use for metaphors
it's all about the food offering and charming

the female. A lizard and parading of feathers may charm
her back! At the Opera the postman runs
his stationery bike on stage, learns to write metaphors

from Neruda to lure his love interest metaphorically.
Her smile is like a butterfly! Our friend's date gave her a charm
bracelet, gold bling on her wrist, a forerunner

to a metamorphosis: to charm or to run?

Half Sestina

A half-sestina is not the same as a tritina. Half sestinas use the full sestina form of six telutons and start out in the sestina pattern, then end. Three stanzas of the sestina, no envoi. An abrupt end to the form. This may be appropriate for a subject that abruptly ends.

Double Sestina

My mentor Star Black masterd the double sestina form in her book, *Double Time* (sadly, out of print). The double sestina has twelve teleutons and twelve stanzas, using a six-line envoi. To sustain this pattern through a 78 line poem, sometimes also playing with line variations to form patterns, is truly amazing and showcases the beauty of the sestina.

Double Sestina Pattern in Fiction

The sestina is not limited to poetry. Author Alice Mattison's book *In Case We're Separated,* uses the thirteen stories in the book to represent in prose format, the thirteen stanzas of a double sestina. She uses repeated <u>topics </u>instead of repeated<u> words.</u> Her topics repeat themselves and each story includes the following:

> *a glass of water*
> *a sharp point*
> *a cord*
> *a mouth*
> *an exchange*
> and *a map that may be wrong.*

**Exercise 13
Variations**

Play with a variation and write a tritina, half sestina, double sestina, or create your own variation!

The language of poetry can indeed be a very thin disguise, or type of skin, over the skeleton of form. We've walked the labyrinth, and have come back changed. The sestina changes along with the times. I'm sure it will be around for a long time to come.

**Exercise 14
Dear Sestina**

For this last exercise, remember the "Dear Sestina" letters at the beginning of this book? Write your own letter to the sestina. What has it taught you? How is your relationship to the sestina changed after knowing it better?

I invite you to share your experiences with this Sestina Playbook and your sestinas!

Email Jules Nyquist at jules@poetryplayhouse.com or post on the Sestina Playbook facebook page. I invite you to join us virtually or in person at a future sestina class taught by Jules at Jules' Poetry Playhouse. www.poetryplayhouse.com.

Happy sestina writing!

Quoted Sestinas by Book reference

Appetites – 2012 (Beatlick Press)
    Ode to Erica Jong
    Sestina for the Way Social Conservatives Want
        Americans to Have Sex
    American Blackout
    Veronica
    Punk Band Tours the Galaxy

Behind the Volcanoes – 2014 (Beatlick Press)
    A Kind of Courage
    Somewhere

Rolling Sixes Sestinas : An Albuquerque Poets Anthology 2016 (Poetry Playhouse Publications)
    Brewery

Homesick, then - 2017 (Beatlick Press & Poetry Playhouse Publications)
    School
    What is It
    Roses

Atomic Paradise (unpublished)
    Day One
    Radium Girls
    Malan
    North Korea Hwasong-15 Shrine

Single poems:
    Sestina for Susan (Crosstown Poets)
    Dear Dirty Dublin
    Intrepid
    Featheredge (tritina) (in *Offerings for the
        Journey* anthology, 2019)
    Mating Rituals (tritina)

I have used the following books in my sestina classes and recommend them for more insights into the sestina form. Recently there have been two new sestina anthologies that are welcome additions to the body of sestina works.

INDIVIDUAL SESTINAS referenced in Jules' sestina classes (a partial list)

Elizabeth Bishop, "Sestina"
Star Black "House Call" (*Double Time)* double sestina
Ciara Shuttleworth "Sestina" You used to love me
    well/one word each line
Miller Williams' "The Shrinking Lonesome Sestina"
    (telutons with a message, line lengths)
Honor Moore "First Time 1950"*Memoir*, Chicory Blue
    Press, 1988. (obsessive content)
Miller Williams' "The Shrinking Lonesome Sestina"
    (telutons with a message, line lengths)
Jonah Winter's Sestina: Bob (one word for teleutons)
Waldman, Anne. *Baby Breakdown.* "How the Sestina
    (Yawn) Works." The Bobbs-Merrill
    Company, 1970.

BOOKS/ANTHOLOGIES FOR FURTHER READING

Beard Whitlow, Carolyn and Krysl, Marilyn. *Obesession: Sestinas in the Twenty-First Century.* Dartmouth College Press, 2014.

Black, Star. *Double Time*. The Groundwater Press, 1995.

Boland, Eavan and Strand, Mark. *The Making of a Poem, A Norton Anthology of Poetic Forms*. W.W. Norton & Co., 2000.

Cummins, James and Lehman, Dave. *Jim and Dave Defeat the Masked Man*. Illustrated by Archie Rand. Soft Skull Press, 2006.

Cummins, James. *The Whole Truth*. Caregie Mellon University Press, 2003.

Finch, Annie, Editor. *A Formal Feeling Comes, Poems in Form by Contemporary Women*. Story Line Press, 1994.

Mattison, Alice. *In Case We're Separated*. Connected stories in fiction with repeated topics. William Morrow, 2005.

Moore, Honor. *Memoir, poems.* "First Time: 1950." Chicory Blue Press, 1988.

Nester, Daniel. *The Incredible Sestina Anthology*. Write Bloody Publishing, 2013.

Nyquist, Jules. *Appetites.* Beatlick Press, 2012. NM/AZ Book Award finalist

---. *Behind the Volcanoes.* Beatlick Press, 2014. NM/AZ Book Award finalist

----*Homesick, then.* Beatlick Press/Poetry Playhouse Publications, 2017. NM/AZ Book award winner in poetry, 2018.

Nyquist, Jules, Editor. *Rolling Sixes Sestinas, An Albuquerque Poetry Anthology,* (Mikki Aronoff, Megan Baldrige, James Dilworth, Winter Elise, Kate Padilla), Poetry Playhouse Publications, 2016.

Sagan, Miriam, *Unbroken Line, Writing in the Lineage of Poetry,* Sherman Asher Publishing, 1999.

Paquet, Susan. *Barrio Streets*, A six act sestina mystery. Chapbook.